SMART ART

Learning to Classify and Critique Art

**Patricia Hollingsworth, Ed.D.,
& Stephen F. Hollingsworth**

Zephyr
Press

REACHING THEIR HIGHEST POTENTIAL

P.O. Box 66006
Tucson, AZ 85728-6006

ABOUT THE AUTHORS

Patricia Hollingsworth, Ed.D., is the director of University School at the University of Tulsa. She has been with the school since 1982 and is a member of the board of directors of the National Association for Gifted Children. She has delivered presentations and published books and articles nationally and internationally. She is coauthor of *Kinetic Kaleidoscope,* a book about movement and the arts. She directed the Center for Arts and Sciences, which was funded by a U.S. Department of Education Javits grant; the center conducted teacher training and curriculum development.

Stephen Hollingsworth graduated from the University of Oregon with a degree in theater and from the University of Tulsa with a degree in electrical engineering. He has given *Smart Art* presentations in the United States, Canada, and Mexico.

Illustrations: Patricia Hollingsworth
Book and cover design: Kathleen Koopman
Editor: Susan Newcomer

Front Cover: *Pittsburgh* by Frank Stella, University of Oregon Museum of Art, Eugene

© 1989 Zephyr Press, Tucson, AZ

ISBN 0-913705-31-4

CONTENTS

Art Reproductions (in order of appearance):

Prints of artwork from the National Gallery may be purchased inexpensively by writing for a catalog to Publications Services, National Gallery of Art, Washington, D.C. 20565.

Slides of artwork from the University of Oregon Museum of Art may be purchased by writing to the University of Oregon Museum of Art, Eugene, Oregon 97403.

INTRODUCTION

Brain research tells us that all parts of the brain are interconnected and interdependent. As Howard Gardner and others have made us keenly aware, there are many types of intelligence and they can all be expanded. When you develop your visual-spatial intelligence, you development many parts of your brain. As you learn the nonverbal ways artists express feelings, moods, and concepts, you develop new ways to find meaning in life. This book can help you expand the visual-spatial intelligence by developing the appreciation of a variety of art.

I remember as a child attending a wedding reception at which I was offered a beautiful pink square of cake that had a small, delicate rosebud on it. I carefully bit into the rose. I was horrified; it was not icing! It was much later that I learned to like cream cheese.

People who expect art to imitate life often have the same reaction when they see an abstract by Picasso or Mondrian. I would never have learned to like cream cheese if I kept expecting icing; people will never learn to appreciate all forms of art if they keep expecting realism.

To appreciate art, we need new ways of seeing it and new ways of talking about what we see. In *Smart Art,* you take an imaginary walk through an art gallery. You learn one way of looking at and talking about art. Obviously, it is not the only way to enjoy art, but it is a way that many students and adults find informative and fun.

You first learn to classify art according to primary purposes. Then you learn to critique art works by following a few simple steps. Finally, using a classification system you develop and information you gather, you form a reasoned opinion about the work. The activities section has exercises that will sharpen your newly learned skills.

Working through *Smart Art* will make you comfortable with classifying and critiquing art and helping others do the same. You will be able to use these skills to assess any artwork you come across. If you want to know more about art, you will find *Smart Art* extremely useful.

I hope you enjoy your visit to the imaginary art gallery! You can astonish your friends and neighbors with your new skills, as well as begin to build a lasting relationship with the enchanting world of art and creativity.

Pat Hollingsworth
email: hollingspl@centum.utulsa.edu

ART CATEGORIES, CRITICISM, AND APPRECIATION

"I don't know anything about art!" This is a typical lament of both teachers and parents when they consider helping children learn to appreciate art. Yet a few simple principles can make art criticism accessible to nearly everyone.

Art criticism simply means talking about art. One learns to defer judgment until one has looked closely at a work of art and followed a few simple steps of critical investigation. Instead of quickly dismissing a work, without taking time to think about the artist's purpose or method, one learns to appreciate the work on its own terms.

Discovering the Purpose of Art

Generally, artists create art for one of three reasons. One, they want to recreate the physical world as they see it. Two, they want to express an idea or feeling. Or three, they want to create an interesting design. Trying to discern the primary purpose of a work of art not only makes for an interesting discussion, but also lays the foundation for evaluating the work.

Art categories are not ironclad, of course, and some works may blur the boundaries between categories. For general purposes, however, the following three categories are useful.

Imitationalism

Some works of art are meant to look like the world around us, much like a photograph. Much of the work of Winslow Homer could be classified as imitationalism. Imitationalism is the type of art that most people can identify with and enjoy. Indeeed, for most people, this IS art. The work looks like the real world as we know it. Most people feel comfortable with this kind of art. The term imitationalism is used because this type of work seeks to *imitate* the world around us. Other terms for imitationalism include realism, representationalism, and naturalism.

Emotionalism

While imitationalism shows us the world we see with our eyes, emotionalism shows us an interior world we cannot see. Emotionalism renders the world of ideas, feelings, moods, fantasy, emotions. The works of Chagall, El Greco, Van Gogh, and Dali fall into this category, as would most religious paintings. Artwork classified as emotionalism may range from realistic to abstract, but the primary purpose of the work is to express strong feelings and the primary impact of the work is *emotional*, thus the term emotionalism. Other terms for emotionalism include expressivism and instrumentalism.

Formalism

Most artists are concerned with the design of the work they create. For some artists, however, creating the design is the primary purpose of the work. They are concerned with the formal qualities of art, the lines, shapes, colors, and textures and how they are arranged on the page. Most of the work of Braque and Mondrian could be classified as formalism. Sometimes recognizable objects appear in formalist paintings, such as in the work of Matisse, but the primary purpose of the objects is to create a visually interesting composition. The artist may use objects from the world as we see it, but these objects are chosen for their *formal* qualities, for the form they take in the work, thus the term formalism. In the work of Matisse, one can recognize flowers, people, doors, windows, tables, but the objects are used to create an interesting composition.

The first step in learning to appreciate art is learning to classify a work according to its primary purpose. Using these categories is somewhat like eating apples and onions. A perfectly good onion will never taste good to a person who expects it to be an apple. The same is true for a work of art in one category that is judged in terms of another category. A person will never learn to appreciate formalism if he or she expects it to look like the real world. Apples need to be judged by apple standards, and onions by onion standards.

Once we have classified a work of art, we are ready to critique it.

Learning to Talk about Art

Critiquing art is like solving a mystery, except the process of investigation is as important as the solution! The work of art will be the mystery. Following four simple steps, we will look at the clues the artist has provided to help us learn more about the work. The first two steps—describing the art elements and analyzing the design—involve looking for clues. In the third step—interpreting the meaning—we try to discover what the clues mean, and in the fourth step—judging the work—we evaluate the work according to what we have found.

Step 1: Describing the Art Elements

In making a work of art, every artist uses a few basic elements: lines, shapes, colors, textures. These can be thought of as clues. In Step 1 of critiquing art, we describe the art elements in the work of art. Lines that are sharp, jagged, and heavy, for example, will convey a different feeling from lines that are soft, graceful, and horizontal. A hard-edged triangle will give a different feeling than a soft-edged circle. Different textures similarly convey different feelings. Colors are also critical. Warm colors are reds, oranges, and yellows. Cool colors are blues and greens. Neutral colors are browns, grays, and whites. Each conveys a different feeling. In Step 1, each art element is examined for the message or clue it conveys about the work of art.

Step 2: Analyzing the Design

In Step 2, we look at how the art elements are put together. A system is a set of interrelated parts designed to create a whole, and as such, the whole is greater than the sum of its parts. A work of art can be thought of as a system in which all the parts, or art elements, are essential in creating the whole. The way the elements are put together or arranged is called the organization, composition, or design. In Step 2, we analyze the design of the work of art. The principles of design include repetition, variation, proximity, focal point, balance, space, and dark and light. These will be further explained in the following pages, but as an example of design, an artist may create rhythm in a work by repeating an element such as line or color. An artist may bring elements together in the work or keep them entirely separate, and a symmetrical design, in which the art elements in each half of the work are in balance, gives a greater sense of stability than an asymmetrical design. In Step 2 we analyze the design of the work in terms of each of the design principles. This gives us further clues to the meaning of the work.

Step 3: Interpreting the Meaning

In Step 3, we look at what we have discovered about the art elements and the design and try to establish the meaning of the work. A work of art can have many meanings, of course, but for the observant investigator, one meaning will stand out as paramount. In this step you ask why. Why is the sky dark? Why are the lines jagged? Why is the balance asymmetrical? This is the time to encourage insight and brainstorming using the information that has been gathered.

Step 4: Judging the Work

After examining the art elements, analyzing the design, and interpreting the meaning, you are ready to judge the work of art. You are now ready to make an informed evaluation of how well the artist has succeeded with his or her work. In Step 4, recall the category in which you originally classified the work and judge how well the artist has succeeded. If you have decided that a work is an example of emotionalism, now decide if it is a successful example of emotionalism. Does it do a credible job of expressing emotion? Judge the work by the standards appropriate to its classification. If the work is an example of formalism, ask if it is successful in creating an interesting composition that makes you aware of the visual elements of line, shape, color, or texture, not whether it looks like something in the real world. Finally, defer judgment no longer. You may decide that a work is an excellent example of emotionalism, but still you may not like it. Or you may love it. In Step 4, you get to choose. Regardless of your final judgment, however, you will have conducted a thorough investigation and, like it or not, will have a greater appreciation of the artwork, the artist, and the process of creativity.

How To Use This Book

Using the simple methods discussed here and expanded in the following pages, you can help children and yourself begin to appreciate art. **SMART ART** makes it easy.

In **SMART ART** you will find:
- **Instructions for Teachers** with suggestions and guidelines for teachers and parents.
- **Talking about Art,** an introductory cartoon about three characters who pay a visit to an imaginary art museum. The three characters have very different ideas about art, but in the museum they gradually come to appreciate other ways of looking at art.
- **Workbook** activities to help students sharpen their skills at classifying and critiquing art.
- **More Activities in Art Criticism** with more art reproductions and questions for looking, thinking, and talking about art.
- A sample **Smart Art Worksheet** that may be reproduced and used as a guide in other art investigations beyond this book.
- A **glossary** that defines art terms with which you may not be familiar.

Using **SMART ART** is easy. First, read this essay again. Once you understand the principles explained here, review the Instructions for Teachers for additional help in how to proceed with students. You are now ready to begin.

Reproduce the cartoon Talking about Art for students and read through it with them carefully. The cartoon characters will help them understand the principles of art criticism. You may want to lead a discussion about the cartoon, the characters, and the ideas expressed. Although the cartoon unfolds effortlessly, the ideas are actually quite advanced, so you will need to help students explore them thoroughly.

With this introduction, you can begin to work through the workbook activities. Each section contains some explanatory material and a variety of exercises. The Instructions for Teachers will explain some of this material further and suggest ways to approach these activities in the classroom.

In the first few exercises, students will be asked to classify different works of art. Sometimes it is difficult to decide which category is best, but how exciting to have a heated discussion about art!

The exercises will then ask students to critique various works of art. Have students think of themselves as detectives searching for clues. You may want to write down the clues as they are discovered. These are excellent activities to develop vocabulary and visual perception. If a child is visually handicapped, exercises can be adapted using a piece of sculpture or collage. The final exercises ask students to interpret the meaning of a work of art and make a judgment. An interesting discussion can ensue during these exercises, and everyone will have an opinion!

Last Word

As you do these activities, remember: the workbook pages are meant only to guide activities. Additional exercises, games, and activities can be developed to expand each section and help explain each principle.

Finally, although the process of art criticism has been likened to solving a mystery, replete with investigators and clues, a work of art is never really "solved" the way great and small crimes are. In general, there are no right or wrong answers, although some opinions may be more reasoned than others, may be based on more evidence than others, or may show more insight than others. But the point is not to solve a mystery but to appreciate the investigation, to question, discuss, debate, learn, and enjoy. This is art criticism at its best, and an ideal introduction to the enthralling world of creativity.

INSTRUCTIONS FOR TEACHERS

Preliminary Words

As you begin to work through **SMART ART** with students, remember that the point of the exercises is to get students to look at art carefully, to think about art creatively, and to talk about art comfortably. Interesting discussions are more important than answers!

Artwork

To do the exercises in **SMART ART**, students will need to look at works of art! It will be more informative to lead class discussions using large color art reproductions available from your local museum, library, or district resource center. Use an easel to position them in front of the room where all can see. You may also find good color reproductions in art books or as posters, slides, or postcards available from museum gift shops and mail-order catalogs. (See p. 4 for more information on ordering the prints appearing in this book.) When choosing works to study, be sure to select ones that have good color and high-quality printing. More exposure to artwork helps students become used to looking at art, so consider using a bulletin board to create a space to display art postcards and other art-related items.

Photocopying SMART ART

Of course, you are also encouraged to photocopy the artwork appearing in **SMART ART** for use in your own classroom. The book is designed for you to photocopy a section or more at a time—enough copies for each student—and to work through the pages as a group, completing the readings and activities on each page and discussing each concept.

Group Discussion

The workbook activities will be more interesting if done in a group. Use the questions in More Activities as a basis for a group discussion when looking at art in this book, the classroom, or a museum.

Extra Paper and Drawing Materials

Some space has been provided after each exercise for answering questions and doing drawings. It is highly recommended that students have available large, separate sheets of paper and crayons, colored pencils, chalk, or paint. Any kind of paper is acceptable, even scrap paper or newsprint or lined paper. This will allow students as much room for expression as possible and preserve the pages of the book for future use.

Start with the Familiar

When beginning a new section or concept, start the discussion with what is familiar—the classroom, for example! Explore new art concepts with students by having them see what is immediately around them. Look around the room to discover lines, shapes, colors, and textures and allow students to point out examples in the room before moving ahead in the book.

First Scan the Artwork

When it is time to begin looking at a work of art, have your class spend a few minutes simply looking at the work. Ask your students to make general observations about the color, the shapes, the impression it creates. Much can be learned from this initial, non-directed observation. You may also want to ask leading questions to bring students into the work, for example, what kinds of lines do you see? Where do they begin? Where do they end? Are they thick or thin?

Minitests

There are minitests in **SMART ART** designed to help students gauge their progress in learning how to talk about art. As you work from section to section, encourage students to build on the concepts they have already learned.

Further Specific Instructions

Step 1: Describing the Art Elements

p. 36. Before beginning to discuss lines in a painting, ask students to look around the classroom and point out lines they see. Ask probing questions to help them see the many possibilities. For example, the shadow under a window sill can represent a line, as does a line printed on a calendar on the wall or the edge of a desk or the folds of a curtain.

p. 45. To introduce color, bring a prism to class and show students how light passing through a prism is refracted into many colors. You may want to complete a color wheel for the class on a large sheet of paper and hang it on the wall.

p. 51. You may want to make collages with students to give them hands-on experience with texture. Have students bring in small scraps of cloth, paper, string, yarn, and other objects and show them how to glue the scraps to a piece of sturdy paper. Ask students to give some thought to how the items are arranged and how the texture of each item contributes to the feel of the collage.

Step 2: Analyzing the Design

p. 57. Students are probably familiar with many kinds of systems, although they may not call them by that name. The point of this discussion is to help students understand what a system is, to help them recognize familiar objects as systems, and to help them see how a work of art can be thought of as a system.

p. 58. Students may need help with the second activity on this page. You may need to suggest other systems with changing parts: for example, a car (seats, body, engine, tires, transmission), a bicycle (seat, handlebars, pedals, wheels), a skateboard (wheels, bearings, axle, platform). Remind them to imagine what these systems would be like if one part was lost or broken.

p. 59. Here we talk about the design of a work of art, but almost everything has a design, either made or naturally occurring. Some objects are designed to look attractive. Others are designed to be strong, functional, or fast. In every case, design is still achieved by arranging the parts in a specific way. Before moving on to discuss works of art, ask students to think about other kinds of design and what purpose each accomplishes. As students begin the activity on this page, encourage them to create designs in which the four elements relate to one another. This will help to visually unify their drawings. In other words, it will make the drawings more like systems, rather than a number of separate parts.

Step 3: Interpreting the Meaning

p. 91. If at all possible, make copies of the Smart Art Worksheet (pp. 107-109) for students to use. Otherwise, have them use a separate sheet of paper for their answers.

Talking about Art: Apples, Onions, and Art Criticism

You are about to share an odd adventure with three imaginary creatures—King Louis the Lion, Mr. Hardy, and Mademoiselle Valerie. They live in the famous foliage of Henri Rousseau's painting *The Equatorial Jungle.*

The three characters have very different ideas about art. King Louis prefers art that has an interesting design. Mr. Hardy prefers art that expresses emotion. Mademoiselle Valerie appreciates only artistic realism, art that imitates the physical world.

One afternoon, they visit a museum, staffed by famous art personages—Leonardo da Vinci's *Mona Lisa* and Rodin's *The Thinker*. As they walk through the museum they discuss several well-known works of art and discover . . . .

Well, enough introduction. Let's turn to the cartoon and see what happens. By the way, below is a relative of King Louis, whom you will meet on the next page.

A Lion, c. 1614-15
Peter Paul Rubens

National Gallery of Art
Washington, D. C.

APPLES, ONIONS, AND ART CRITICISM

Once upon a time there were three dwellers in the Deep Forest. They were happy there and almost never fought or quarreled with each other until one day . . .

They bicycle to the museum, which is in a clearing.

They walk into the museum and go to the information desk.

Still Life with Fish, 1908
William Merritt Chase

University of Oregon Museum of Art
Eugene

Grieving, n.d.   University of Oregon Museum of Art
Leonard Baskin   Eugene

Pittsburgh, 1933-43
Frank Stella

University of Oregon Museum of Art
Eugene

Look at this one! It doesn't look like anything at all!

No, it doesn't, but I like it! It gives me a feeling of excitement, fast cars, big planes, and skyscrapers! But it certainly doesn't look real.

It's not supposed to look real. This kind of art is called **formalism** because its main purpose is to create an interesting design. This is the kind of art I like. It is worthy of a king! The swirls, arcs, and crisscrossing shapes all create a masterful pattern!

Apples, Onions, and Art Criticism 21

Still Life with Fish, 1908   University of Oregon Museum of Art
William Merritt Chase   Eugene

Pittsburgh, 1933-43   University of Oregon Museum of Art
Frank Stella   Eugene

According to the guidebook, we are all right!
If the primary purpose of a work of art is to
imitate the real world, then it is called **imitationalism**.

But if the primary purpose of a work is
to express strong emotion,
then it is called **emotionalism**.

Grieving, n.d.   University of Oregon Museum of Art
Leonard Baskin   Eugene

And if the primary purpose of a work
is to arrange lines, shapes, colors,
and textures, that is called **formalism**.

Let's start by investigating this one. First of all, the only color is black and white. That's our first clue.

In front, there's a person on a bridge holding his hands up to his ears. His mouth is open in a long oval shape, his eyes are wide open, and his face looks like a skull. His body makes a kind of S-shape and blends in somewhat with the bridge. And it may be a woman, not a man. There are two other figures at the other end of the bridge, perhaps looking the other way.

The Scream, 1895
Edvard Munch

National Gallery of Art
Washington, D.C.

I see both thick and thin black lines going up, down, and diagonally in wavy, swimmy patterns. In the back there are two small islands with trees or crosses on them.

The Scream, 1895
Edvard Munch

National Gallery of Art
Washington, D.C.

So, now we've completed Step 1. We've described the lines, shapes, and colors in this picture. What does the guidebook say about the next step?

In Step 2 we **analyze** the design of the painting. We look at how the lines, shapes, and colors are put together. The design will give us additional clues to the meaning of the work.

Well, what stands out most in the painting is the person's face! It's in the center of the painting, and the white color against the black lines makes the head stand out above all.

Pat Hollingsworth

The Scream, 1895
Edvard Munch

National Gallery of Art
Washington, D.C.

Workbook: Activities in Classifying and Critiquing Art

This part of **SMART ART** contains a number of activities to help you sharpen your skills at classifying and critiquing art. The exercises require you to think, draw, and write. Hope you have more fun than Dürer's knight!

Knight, Death and the Devil, 1513
Albrecht Dürer

National Gallery of Art
Washington, D.C.

CLASSIFYING ART

ART CATEGORIES

Most artists have a primary reason for creating their art, and most works of art can be classified according to their primary purpose. The first step in art criticism is to classify a work of art. In **SMART ART**, you will be using three categories:

Imitationalism is the category used for works of art that try to imitate the real world as we see it, much like a photograph.

Emotionalism is the category used for works of art that try to express strong emotion. The artist is expressing things we cannot see but things we feel, think, or imagine.

Formalism is the category used for works of art concerned with the pattern of lines, colors, shapes, and textures. The artist is concerned primarily with the design of the work.

On a separate piece of paper, draw your own example of the three art categories.
Imitationalism: Select an object from real life to draw.
Emotionalism: Create a drawing to express one particular feeling.
Formalism: Create an interesting design using lines, shapes, and colors.

NOTE: This symbol signals an art activity designed to help you practice what you have been learning in **SMART ART**.

For each of the six works of art that follow, decide which art category best describes its primary purpose. Circle your answer.

Oysters, 1862
Edouard Manet

National Gallery of Art
Washington, D.C.

IMITATIONALISM   EMOTIONALISM   FORMALISM

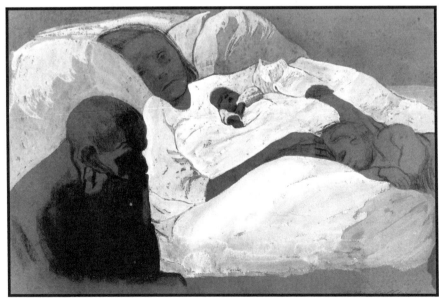

Unemployment, 1909
Käthe Kollwitz

National Gallery of Art
Washington, D.C.

IMITATIONALISM   EMOTIONALISM   FORMALISM

The Old Violin, c. 1890
John Frederick Peto

National Gallery of Art
Washington, D.C.

IMITATIONALISM   EMOTIONALISM   FORMALISM

Zirchow VII, 1918
Lyonel Feininger

National Gallery of Art
Washington, D.C.

IMITATIONALISM   EMOTIONALISM   FORMALISM

The Prophet, 1912
Emil Nolde

National Gallery of Art
Washington, D.C.

IMITATIONALISM   EMOTIONALISM   FORMALISM

Diamond Painting in Red, Yellow, Blue, c. 1921-25
Piet Mondrian

National Gallery of Art
Washington, D.C.

IMITATIONALISM   EMOTIONALISM   FORMALISM

For answers, see key on p. 112.

ART CATEGORIES

 Below is a chart you can use to keep track of the works of art you see. Select artwork in this book or elsewhere. Write the date you saw it, the title, the artist, where you saw it, and the art category that best describes it. Some of the work may not be easy to categorize. You may decide that some works belong to more than one category. You may want to complete this chart over a period of time.

Date	Title	Artist	Place	Category

CRITIQUING ART

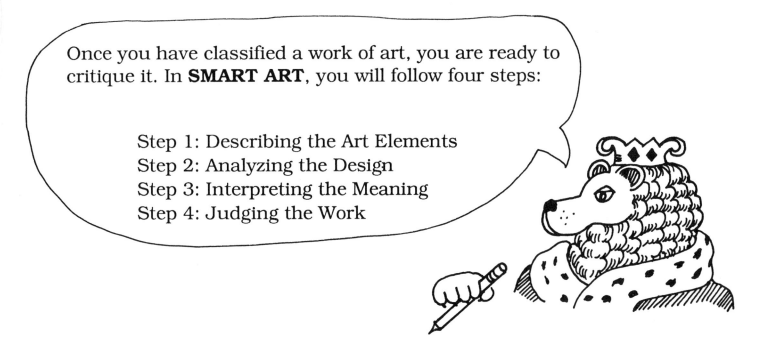

Once you have classified a work of art, you are ready to critique it. In **SMART ART**, you will follow four steps:

Step 1: Describing the Art Elements
Step 2: Analyzing the Design
Step 3: Interpreting the Meaning
Step 4: Judging the Work

Step 1: Describing the Art Elements

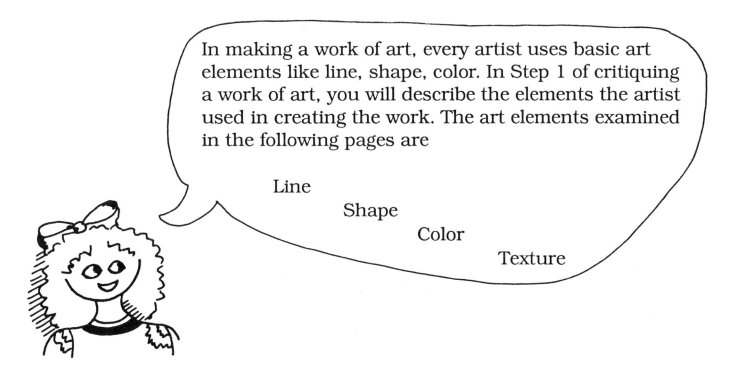

In making a work of art, every artist uses basic art elements like line, shape, color. In Step 1 of critiquing a work of art, you will describe the elements the artist used in creating the work. The art elements examined in the following pages are

Line

Shape

Color

Texture

LINE

*A **line** can be described as a dot moving through space. A line can show the edge of an object.*

Pretend that your pencil or pen point is a dot.
Let it move through the space below.

Lines can be drawn in different ways: thick or thin, straight or curved, wiggly or jagged. Different lines show different effects and say different things. For example, a light line shows softness, a heavy line shows strength, a jagged line shows fear.

Look at the different ways lines have been used to draw the lion below. Use the spaces to describe the type of line used *or* write a word that describes each lion.

_____   _____   _____

Artists use lines in many ways. Now it's your turn to draw some lines.

In the boxes below, draw a line or lines that look . . .

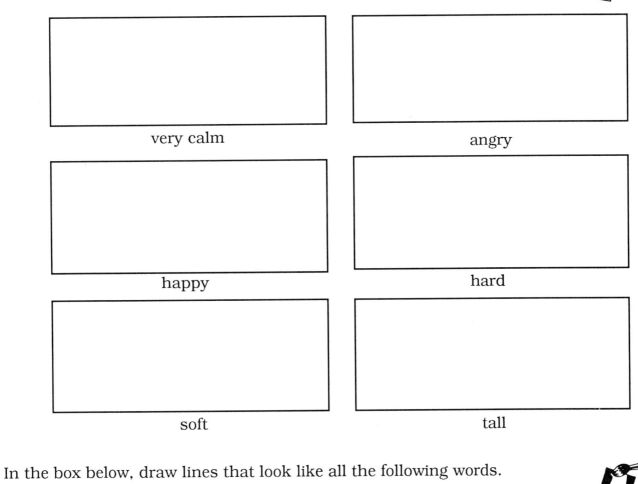

very calm

angry

happy

hard

soft

tall

In the box below, draw lines that look like all the following words.
Overlapping is encouraged!

marching   peaceful   broken   bursting   diagonal

Line

Look at **Grieving** by Leonard Baskin on p. 20. Circle the words that describe the types of lines Baskin used. Add at least 3 of your own.

thick	smooth	nervous
thin	broken	playful
vertical	angular	calm
horizontal	rhythmic	angry
diagonal	choppy	happy
fuzzy	graceful	sad
jagged	careful	tall
loose	lazy	short

_____ _____ _____

Using the 2 works of art listed below, copy 4 lines you see used in each and choose a word to describe each line.

A Lion by Peter Paul Rubens on p.13.		**Knight, Death and the Devil** by Albrecht Dürer on p. 29.	
Draw the lines here:	Write a word to describe them here:	Draw the lines here:	Write a word to describe them here:
1.	1. _____	1.	1. _____
2.	2. _____	2.	2. _____
3.	3. _____	3.	3. _____
4.	4. _____	4.	4. _____

✐ Which art category best describes **A Lion**?
IMITATIONALISM EMOTIONALISM FORMALISM

✐ Which art category best describes **Knight, Death and the Devil**?
IMITATIONALISM EMOTIONALISM FORMALISM

SHAPE

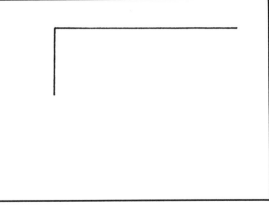

*When a line encloses an area, it is called a **shape**. When a line separates one area from another, it creates a **shape**.*

In the spaces below, put your pencil point at the end of each line and continue the line until you make a shape.

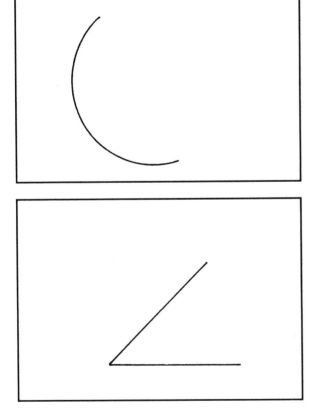

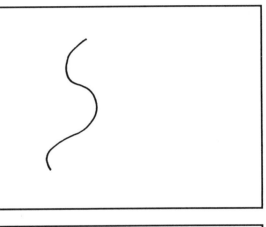

Shapes can be drawn in different ways to show different things. Some shapes define objects such as a cup, a table, or a head. Some shapes express or convey ideas such as wholeness, balance, or distance.

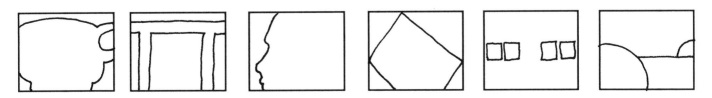

Shape

Artists use shapes in many ways.
Now it's your turn to draw some shapes.

In the boxes below, draw a shape or shapes that look . . .

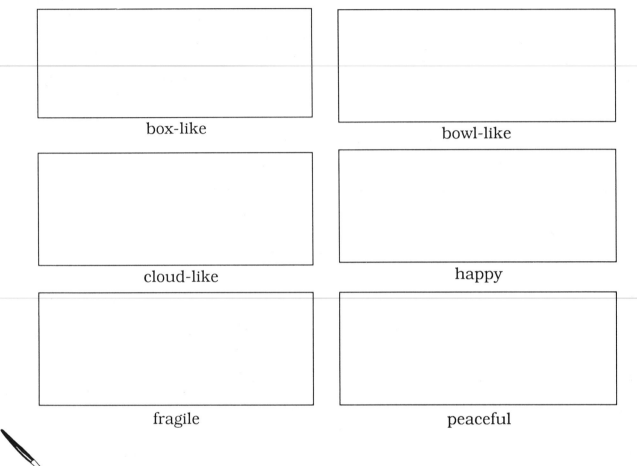

box-like

bowl-like

cloud-like

happy

fragile

peaceful

In the box below, draw shapes that look like all the following words.
Overlapping is encouraged!

rising   flat   divided   puffy   silly

Look at **The Boating Party** by Mary Cassatt on p. 42.

1. Look at the shapes of the man, the woman, and the child. Use 2 words to describe each of these shapes.

man _____ , _____

woman _____ , _____

child _____ , _____

2. Look at the shapes of the boat, the oar, the sail, and the seats. Use 2 words to describe each of these shapes.

boat_____ , _____

oar _____ , _____

sail _____ , _____

seats_____ , _____

3. Are there other shapes in the painting? Where are they? Describe them.

4. Turn the painting upside down and look at it from a distance (or squint). What new shapes appear?

5. Can you now see that this painting is an arrangement of shapes as well as a picture of a boating party?

The Boating Party, 1893-94
Mary Cassatt

National Gallery of Art
Washington, D.C.

6. Make several copies of the outline of **The Boating Party** on p. 44.

  • On one copy, fill in the shapes using 2 colors.
  • On another copy, fill in the shapes using 4 colors.
  • On a third, use only black and white.

  Look at the differences between the drawings. Did color change the feeling of the shapes?

7. Now, look at the painting again. Do you see how Mary Cassatt and other artists use shapes to make a picture?

✎ Which art category best describes **The Boating Party**?
    IMITATIONALISM   EMOTIONALISM   FORMALISM

Name That Shape!
An activity for two or more players.

This exercise will improve your ability to talk about art. It will also encourage creative listening.

  • One person needs a pencil and a piece of paper. The other person needs to select a reproduction of a work of art but not show it to his or her partner.
  • The person with the reproduction describes the shapes and spaces. Do not say what the shapes represent. Remember the words you have learned so far in talking about shapes.
  • The person with the pencil and paper draws what is described. Take your time and listen carefully.
  • When finished, compare your drawing with the reproduction!
  • Now, the partners can switch roles and do it again with a new reproduction.

44   Step 1: Describing the Art Elements

CRITIQUING ART
Step 1: Describing the Art Elements

> **Color** is the way we see light reflected from a surface or refracted through a prism.

Artists sometimes think of colors as arranged in a circle—or on a wheel. This makes it easy to see all the colors and how they relate to each other. On the following page is a wheel you can use to create your own color wheel.

• The first step in creating a color wheel is to insert the **primary** colors. The primary colors are red, yellow, and blue. They are called primary because all other colors are made from them.

RED   YELLOW   BLUE

Color the primary colors in the circles at the tips of the solid triangle on the color wheel.

• The next step is to insert the **secondary** colors. The secondary colors are purple, green, and orange. They are called secondary colors because they are made from mixing 2 of the primary colors.

PURPLE   GREEN   ORANGE

Use your purple, green, and orange crayons to color in the circles at the tips of the broken triangle on the color wheel. Put the purple between the red and blue circles, the green between the blue and yellow circles, and the orange between the yellow and red circles.

Now you have a color wheel to use!

COLOR WHEEL

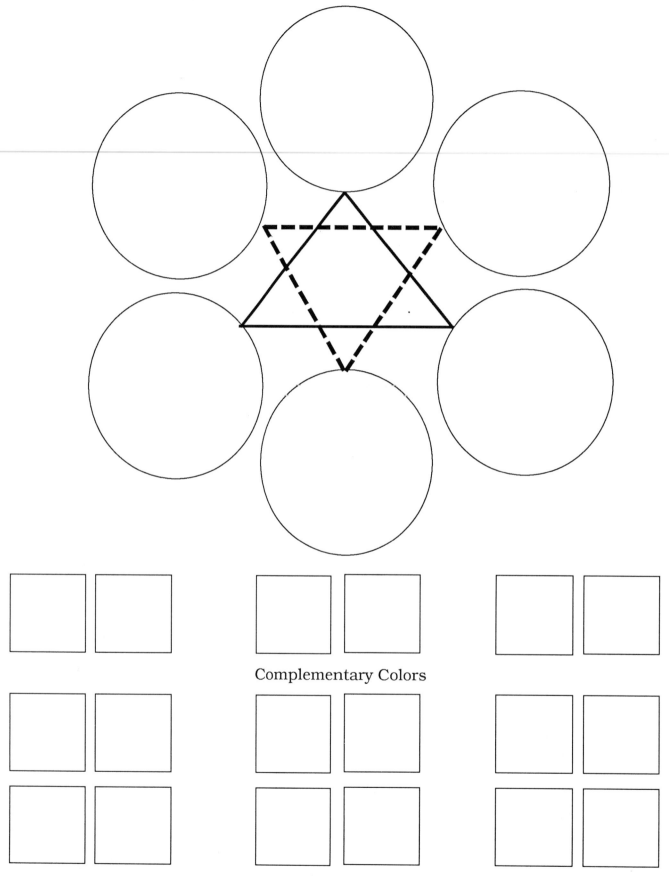

Complementary Colors

Analogous Colors

- **Complementary** colors are colors opposite one another on the wheel. For example:

On the color wheel, find the 3 pairs of complementary colors and color them in the spaces provided below the wheel.

- **Analogous** colors are colors next to each other on the color wheel. For example:

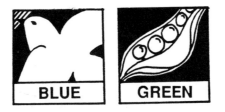

On the color wheel, find the 6 pairs of analogous colors and color them in the spaces provided below the wheel.

Although there are 6 colors on our color wheel, an infinite number of colors can be created by mixing analogous pairs. For example:

yellow + green = yellow green

yellow + yellow green = yellow yellow green

The color wheel can also be divided into **warm** and **cool** colors.

Red, orange, and yellow are usually thought of as warm colors. Why do you think this is so?

Green, blue, and purple are usually thought of as cool colors. Why do you think this is so?

Color

An easy way to remember warm and cool colors is to connect warm colors to warm objects and cool colors to cool objects. Below, connect the object to an appropriate color.

Red	Ocean
Orange	Fire
Green	Shady Tree
Blue	Sun
Purple	Ice Cubes
Yellow	Erupting Volcano

On a separate piece of paper draw a picture of each object and color it the appropriate color.

Warm colors tend to look as if they are closer to you, while cool colors look farther away. Some people say that warm colors **advance** and cool colors **recede**.

Look at **Riverside Picnic** by Vernon Witham on the back cover. Which objects look closest to the viewer? What colors are they?

objects   colors

_____   _____

_____   _____

Which objects look farthest away? What colors are they?

objects   colors

_____   _____

_____   _____

Here are some more color words.

Pigment: substances used to give color. Originally, pigments included natural materials like walnut shells, carrots, and berries. Today, most pigments are manufactured.

Hue: another name for color. For example, red, red-orange, orange, orange-yellow, yellow, yellow-green, and green are all hues.

Intensity: the brightness of a color. A color will appear brighter when placed next to its complement.

Value: the lightness or darkness of a color. Lightness is achieved by adding white to a color. This is called a **tint**. Darkness is achieved by adding black to a color. This is called a **shade**.

Use 4 pieces of poster paper and tempera, acrylic, or water color paints to create 4 paintings by using the following:

• 1 color and 1 shape

• 2 complementary colors and 2 shapes

• 2 analogous colors and 3 shapes

• 2 warm or 2 cool colors and any number of shapes

Now, look at each painting and give it a title. Show your work to other students and explain why you chose your title.

Find a large color reproduction or use one from the front or back cover of this book. Look at it carefully and answer the following questions.

Title _____   Name of artist _____

Check the kinds of colors you see and name them.

     ☐ primary   _____, _____, _____

     ☐ secondary   _____, _____, _____

     ☐ analogous   _____, _____, _____

     ☐ complementary   _____, _____, _____

     ☐ warm   _____, _____, _____

     ☐ cool   _____, _____, _____

     ☐ shades   _____, _____, _____

     ☐ tints   _____, _____, _____

     ☐ advancing   _____, _____, _____

     ☐ receding   _____, _____, _____

Why did the artist use these kinds of colors?

_____ to imitate the world _____ to create a feeling, mood, or idea

_____ to create an interesting form or design

CRITIQUING ART
Step 1: Describing the Art Elements

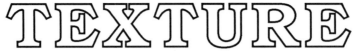

(**Texture** *refers to the way a surface feels or looks like it feels.*)

There are two kinds of texture: tactile texture and visual texture.

The way a surface really feels is called **tactile texture**. "Tactile" means relating to the sense of touch. Every surface has a texture. You can feel texture all around you.

There are many kinds of textures:

smooth   rough   bumpy   slippery

 Point out some of the following textures in the classroom or at home. Write where you saw each one in the spaces provided:

coarse _____ _____   scratchy _____ _____

slick _____ _____   layered _____ _____

sandy _____ _____   soft _____ _____

ribbed _____ _____   furry _____ _____

velvety _____ _____   polished _____ _____

In art, tactile textures are used in a variety of ways. One, for example, is an **impasto**, created when paint is applied so heavily that is stands up in lumps.

Another example is a **collage**, which is created by pasting together paper, cloth, or other materials on a surface. You might make a collage in your classroom or at home.

A third example of tactile texture is a **mosaic**, a work of art made of many pieces of colored tile or stone.

Below are two works of art. If you were in Venice you could really *feel* their texture, but because they are reproduced in this book, you only have the *illusion* of texture. Visual texture refers to that illusion: the way a surface looks like it would feel although the surface is smooth.

The Apostle   Cathedral of San Marcos
Venice, Italy

Madonna and Child   Cathedral of San Marcos
Venice, Italy

Texture

Look through magazines and cut out as many examples of visual texture as you can find. Paste some of them on a separate sheet of paper and label them with a 1-word description.

Artists often create the illusion of texture.

Look at **Still Life** by Henri Fantin-Latour on p. 53. List all the textures you see in this painting. (Find at least 10.)

pulp of orange _____ _____ _____ _____

_____ _____ _____ _____ _____

How many shapes do you see in this painting?

What colors did the artist use?

What effect do the textures, shapes, and colors help create?

✐ Which art category best describes **Still Life**?

IMITATIONALISM   EMOTIONALISM   FORMALISM

Still Life, 1866
Henri Fantin-Latour

Summary

In Step 1 of Critiquing Art we have examined the four elements that artists use in creating a work of art—line, color, shape, and texture. We are almost ready to discuss how these elements are arranged to create a visual whole. But first we will review some of what we have learned.

━━━━━━━━━━━━━━━━━━ **REVIEW** ━━━━━━━━━━━━━━━━━━

Use the words in the box below to answer the following questions. Some words may be used more than once.

1. The four elements an artist uses to create a work of art are _____, _____, _____, and _____,

2. A line can be described as a _____ moving through space.

3. When a line encloses an _____ , it creates a shape.

4. When a line separates one area from another, it creates a _____.

5. Some shapes define objects. Some shapes convey _____, _____, or _____.

6. Color is the way we see _____ reflected from a surface or refracted through a prism.

7. The primary colors are_____, _____, and _____.

8. Green, orange, and purple are called _____ colors because they are made by mixing the _____ colors.

9. Orange and blue are examples of _____ colors. _____ and _____ are also, as are _____ and _____ .

10. Warm colors are usually _____, _____, and _____.

11. Cool colors are usually _____ , _____ , and _____.

12. Name three hues: _____ , _____ , and _____ .

13. What is a pigment found in nature? _____ .

14. The way a surface feels is called _____ texture.

15. A work of art made of many pieces of colored tile or stone is called a _____.

16. _____ texture refers to the way a surface looks like it would feel although it is actually smooth.

WORD BOX

red	line				blue
area	green			wholeness	balance
analogous	complementary	shape	dot	light	orange
visual	mosaic	purple	yellow	intensity	tactile
secondary	distance	primary	color	texture	berries

For answers, see key on p. 112.

Complete the puzzle with words for the art elements shown below. Try to make each letter of the word look like the element named.

1. _____

2. _____
   RED   YELLOW   BLUE

3. _____

4. _____

For answers, see key on p. 112.

CRITIQUING ART
Step 2: Analyzing the Design

The way art elements are put together in a work of art is called the composition or design. In Step 2 of critiquing a work of art, you will analyze an artwork's design. We will begin by discussing two important concepts:

                    System
                    Design

Then we will discuss the principles of design. The principles of design examined in **SMART ART** are

Repetition
        Variation
                Proximity
                        Focal Point
                                Balance
                                        Space
                                                Dark and Light

> *A work of art can be thought of as a **system**.*
> *A system is a set of parts that are combined to*
> *create a whole. The following are systems:*

the human body

the engine of a car

the universe

the ecology of the earth

a tool

Mona Lisa

a sculpture

a building

a song

a camera

a play

a ship

Think about the parts that make each of these systems.

System

Name 4 parts that make each of the following systems:

a tree	_____ ,	_____ ,	_____ ,	_____
a building	_____ ,	_____ ,	_____ ,	_____
a dance	_____ ,	_____ ,	_____ ,	_____
a painting	_____ ,	_____ ,	_____ ,	_____
a sculpture	_____ ,	_____ ,	_____ ,	_____
a song	_____ ,	_____ ,	_____ ,	_____

The parts of a system are **interrelated**. When one part changes, the whole changes.

Name 3 systems. For each system, name 4 parts.

1. _____   2. _____   3. _____

_____   _____   _____

_____   _____   _____

_____   _____   _____

_____   _____   _____

Now change 1 of the 4 parts in each system and describe how the whole system has changed. Here's an example:

system	parts	changed parts	description of change
tree	branches	branches	The tree system has changed
	leaves	leaves	because the flowers have
	trunk	trunk	changed to apples. The season
	flowers	apples	has changed from summer to fall,
			causing the blossoms to form
			fruit.

In the 13th century, St. Thomas Aquinas observed, "The whole is greater than the sum of its parts." What do you think this means?

A work of art can be thought of as a system in which all the parts or art elements create a whole. The way the elements are put together is called the composition or **design**. The design creates a visual unity.

In the box below, create a simple design using the 4 art elements you have already learned.

On the following pages we will examine some principles of design:
repetition
variation
proximity
focal point
balance
space
dark and light

Artists use principles of design to create wholeness or visual unity.

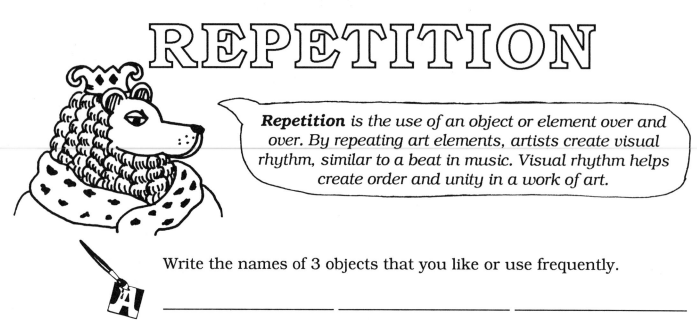

REPETITION

Repetition is the use of an object or element over and over. By repeating art elements, artists create visual rhythm, similar to a beat in music. Visual rhythm helps create order and unity in a work of art.

Write the names of 3 objects that you like or use frequently.

_____ _____ _____

Now select one of these objects to draw. In the space below, create your own design by repeating the object as many times as you wish.

What feeling does the repetition create? Why?

The amount of repetition an artist uses depends on the purpose of the work of art. Repetition can create many effects. For example:

confusion

calmness

By repeating the art elements named below, create the feeling written under the box:

shape

color

line

strength

serenity

fragility

Look at ***The Equatorial Jungle*** by Henri Rousseau on p. 62. In the boxes below, draw the lines you see repeated.

The Equatorial Jungle, 1909
Henri Rousseau

National Gallery of Art
Washington, D.C.

In the boxes below, draw the shapes you see repeated in *The Equatorial Jungle.*

What feelings does the repetition of lines and shapes create in the painting?

✏ Which art category best describes *The Equatorial Jungle?*
IMITATIONALISM   EMOTIONALISM   FORMALISM

Select another work of art from this book that uses repetition.

Title _____   Artist _____

In the space below, describe the art elements that are repeated.

What feelings does the repetition create in the work?

✏ Which art category best describes this painting?
IMITATIONALISM   EMOTIONALISM   FORMALISM

VARIATION

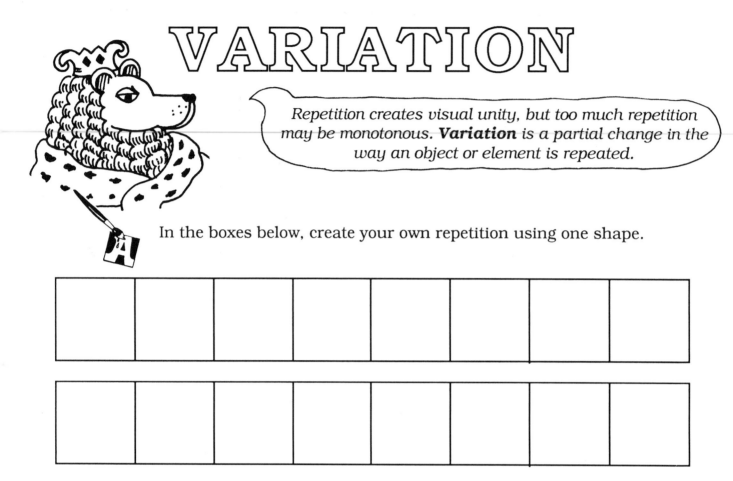

*Repetition creates visual unity, but too much repetition may be monotonous. **Variation** is a partial change in the way an object or element is repeated.*

In the boxes below, create your own repetition using one shape.

Look at what you've just drawn. Now using the same shape, create a variation of this drawing.

All things in nature contain both repetition and variation.

No two leaves are exactly the same.

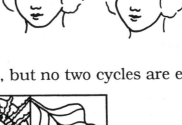

No two human beings are exactly the same.

There is repetition in the cycles of the seasons, but no two cycles are ever alike.

The amount of variation and repetition that an artist uses in a work of art depends on the purpose of the work.

Look at the variation in **Still Life** by Pablo Picasso on p. 66. In the boxes below, draw the lines, shapes, and textures you see.

What effect does the variation create in this painting?

Choose a variety of single words to describe this painting.

_____ _____ _____ _____ _____ _____

✏ Which art category best describes **Still Life**?

IMITATIONALISM   EMOTIONALISM   FORMALISM

Still Life. 1918
Pablo Picasso

National Gallery of Art
Washington, D.C.

66   *Step 2: Analyzing the Design*

Look again at **The Equatorial Jungle** by Henri Rousseau on p. 62. Notice the variation the artist used in the painting. What feeling does this variation create?

What effect does the use of both repetition and variation create?

Look at **My Gems** by William M. Harnett on p. 68. What art elements did the artist vary to make this work exciting?

What art elements did the artist repeat to give this work unity?

✏ Which art category best describes **My Gems**?
IMITATIONALISM   EMOTIONALISM   FORMALISM

My Gems, n.d.
William M. Harnett

National Gallery of Art
Washington, D.C.

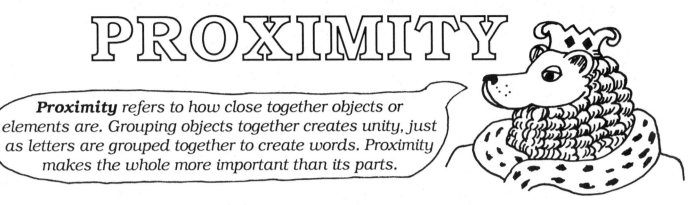

PROXIMITY

Proximity refers to how close together objects or elements are. Grouping objects together creates unity, just as letters are grouped together to create words. Proximity makes the whole more important than its parts.

THESEWORDSAREHARDTOREADBECAUSETHEYARENOTGROUPEDNORMAL

Overlapping is a form of proximity that shows that one object is in front of another.

Draw the objects pictured below showing proximity and overlapping.

proximity   overlapping

Look at *A Corner of the Moulin de la Galette* by Henri de Toulouse-Lautrec on p. 70. Point out two figures that overlap. Which figure appears to be behind *all* the others? How do you know?

✎ Which art category best describes *A Corner of the Moulin de la Galette*?
IMITATIONALISM   EMOTIONALISM   FORMALISM

Look again at *Still Life* by Picasso on p. 66, *My Gems* by Harnett on p. 68, and *A Corner of the Moulin de la Galette* by Toulouse-Lautrec on p. 70. Think about what these paintings have in common.

A Corner of the Moulin de la Galette, 1892
Henri de Toulouse-Lautrec

National Gallery of Art
Washington, D.C.

FOCAL POINT

*The **focal point** is the first thing that attracts your eye to a work of art. It is often what the artist wanted to emphasize most.*

Look at **Self-Portrait** by Rembrandt van Rijn on p. 72. Where is the focal point? How did the artist bring your attention to that place?

☞ Which art category best describes **Self-Portrait**?
IMITATIONALISM   EMOTIONALISM   FORMALISM

Some works of art do not have a focal point. Fabric designs, for example, often do not have a focal point. Artists use focal points, or the lack of focal points, for a purpose.

Draw a patterned fabric design from your own or someone else's clothing.

Is there a focal point in the design? If not, think about why the artist who created the design did not include one.

Look at **Number 1, 1950 (Lavender Mist)** by Jackson Pollock on p. 73. Some people see a focal point in this painting. Others do not. Do you? What is it? Could there be more than one focal point? What effect does an ambiguous focal point create? Think about why the artist titled this **Lavender Mist**.

☞ Which art category best describes **Number 1, 1950 (Lavender Mist)**?
IMITATIONALISM   EMOTIONALISM   FORMALISM

Self-Portrait, 1659
Rembrandt van Rijn

National Gallery of Art
Washington, D.C.

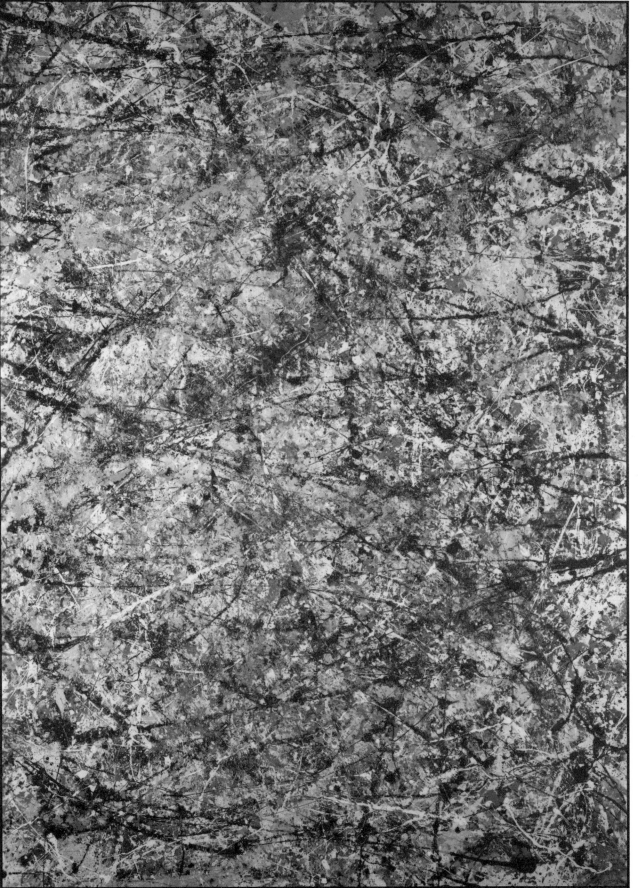

Number 1, 1950 (Lavender Mist), 1950
Jackson Pollock

BALANCE

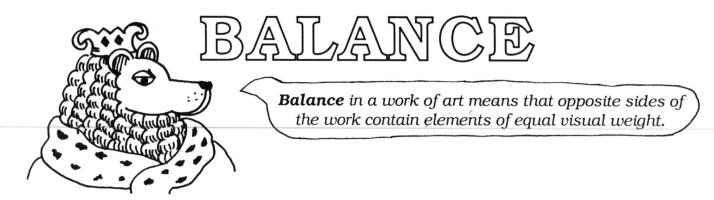

Balance in a work of art means that opposite sides of the work contain elements of equal visual weight.

There are three kinds of balance: symmetrical balance, asymmetrical balance, and radial balance.

Symmetrical balance is achieved when opposite sides of a work of art are balanced by matching elements.

Generally, animal faces and bodies exhibit symmetrical balance. Think about why this is so.

 Fold a piece of paper in half. On one half, draw the outline of one side of a cat's face (or other animal). Keeping the paper folded, cut out your drawing on the line. Open your paper and see a perfect example of symmetrical balance!

Symmetrical balance creates a feeling of stability and permanence. Symmetrical balance is often found in architecture and religious works of art.

Look at *The Visitation of St. Nicholas and St. Anthony Abbott* by Piero di Cosimo on p. 76. Strictly speaking, this painting is only some-what symmetrical. Look closely. On a separate piece of paper, draw all the figures and objects that are on both the right and left sides of this painting. Notice the symmetrical balance in this painting. Think about why symmetry is often used in religious paintings.

✏ Which art category best describes *The Visitation of St. Nicholas and St. Anthony Abbott?*
IMITATIONALISM   EMOTIONALISM   FORMALISM

In **asymmetrical balance**, opposite sides of the work of art are balanced, but not with matching elements. Instead, the work is balanced with elements that attract the eye equally.

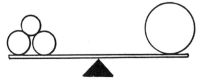

Look at *The Church at Saint-Severin* by Maurice Utrillo on p. 77. Notice the elements that are balanced in this painting. Do other shapes or lines help create balance? Which ones? Compare and contrast the look of symmetrical and asymmetrical paintings. Do you have a preference?

✏ Which art category best describes *The Church at Saint-Severin?*
IMITATIONALISM   EMOTIONALISM   FORMALISM

The Visitation of St. Nicholas and St. Anthony Abbott, c. 1490
Piero di Cosimo

National Gallery of Art
Washington, D.C.

The Church at Saint-Severin, c.1913
Maurice Utrillo

National Gallery of Art
Washington, D.C.

Balance

When a work exhibits **radial balance,** all the elements in the picture branch out in all directions from a common point. Radial balance is often seen in the art of tribal cultures. Radial balance is seen everywhere in nature and in manufactured products.

Draw 3 objects that have radial balance, one each from home, school, and nature.

Look at **Another Time** by Kenneth Noland on p. 79. Does it exhibit radial balance? How? Is the radial balance completely accurate? Why or why not? What effect is created by radial balance?

In the box to the right, draw what Noland's painting would have looked like if it had radial balance in the strictest sense.

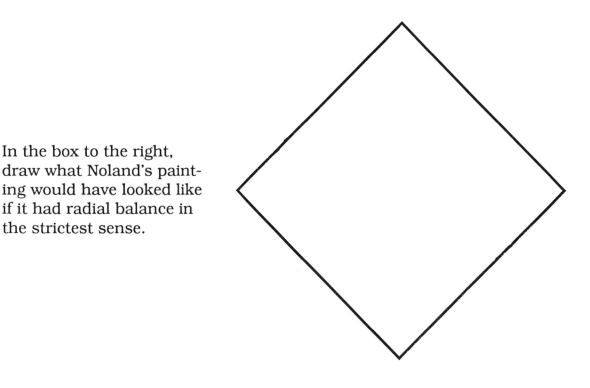

✎ Which art category best describes **Another Time**?
IMITATIONALISM   EMOTIONALISM   FORMALISM

Another Time, 1973
Kenneth Noland

National Gallery of Art
Washington, D.C.

> In art, **space** is the illusion of distance on a flat surface. Some artists create the illusion of great space, as if there is great distance between objects. This is called **deep space**. Some artists create the illusion of little or no space, as if there is no distance between objects. This is called **shallow space**.

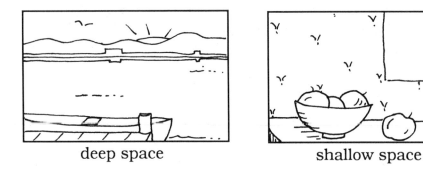

deep space   shallow space

The **foreground** is the part of the artwork that looks closest to the viewer. This is often the most important part of the artwork.

The **background** is the part of the artwork that looks farthest away from the viewer. Walls and sky are often used as backgrounds.

Both the foreground and background are important to the design and the meaning of the artwork.

On a separate piece of paper, create your own drawing using deep space. Put a boat and a dock in the foreground and water, a bridge, and sky in the background of the picture. Begin by drawing the boat close to the bottom of the box. Draw the sky close to the top of the box and the other objects in between.

On a separate piece of paper, create your own drawing using shallow space. Put an apple, a bowl, and a vase with flowers on a table in the foreground and a wall in the background. Begin by drawing the apple close to the bottom of the box and the wall behind all the objects. Remember to use overlapping!

Look at **St. George and the Dragon** by Rogier van der Weyden on p. 82. Notice what is in the foreground. Notice what is a few feet behind St. George. Notice what is just over the rocks behind St. George and what is beyond that in the background. How has the artist created the illusion of so much space on a flat surface?

✏ Which art category best describes **St. George and the Dragon**?
IMITATIONALISM   EMOTIONALISM   FORMALISM

Look at **Self-Portrait** by Paul Gauguin on p. 83. What kind of space is created here? How is this done?

✏ Which art category best describes **Self-Portrait**?
IMITATIONALISM   EMOTIONALISM   FORMALISM

St. George and the Dragon, c. 1432
Rogier van der Weyden

National Gallery of Art
Washington, D.C.

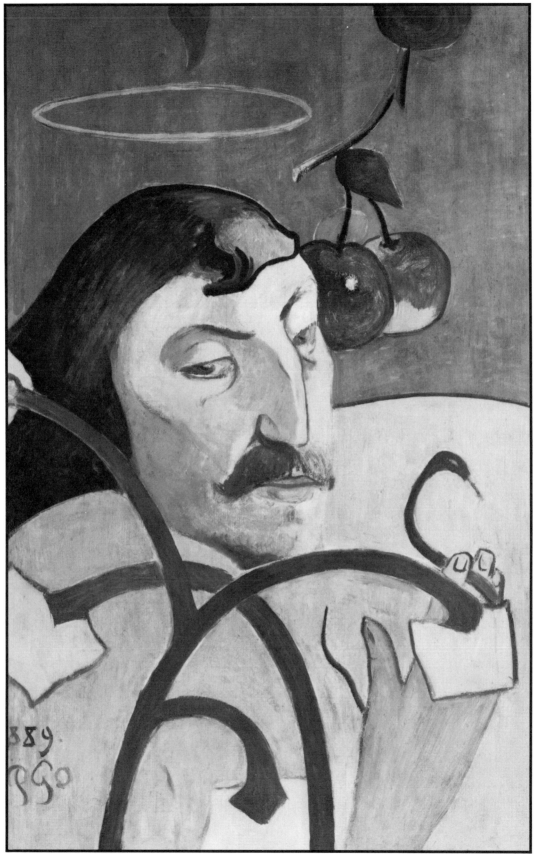

Self-Portrait, 1889
Paul Gauguin

National Gallery of Art
Washington, D.C.

DARK AND LIGHT

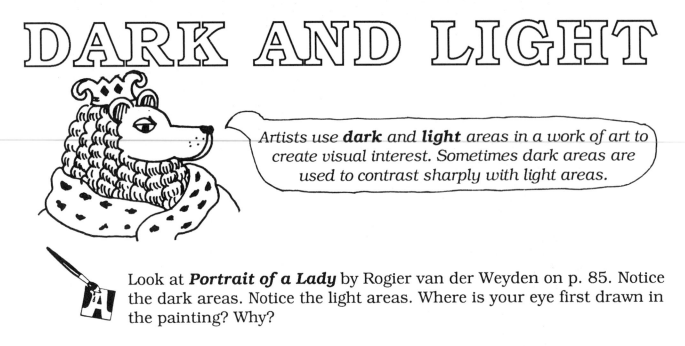

*Artists use **dark** and **light** areas in a work of art to create visual interest. Sometimes dark areas are used to contrast sharply with light areas.*

Look at **Portrait of a Lady** by Rogier van der Weyden on p. 85. Notice the dark areas. Notice the light areas. Where is your eye first drawn in the painting? Why?

✏ Which art category best describes **Portrait of a Lady**?
IMITATIONALISM   EMOTIONALISM   FORMALISM

Dark and light areas are also used to suggest emotion.

Look at **Siegfried and the Rhine Maidens** by Albert Pinkham Ryder on p. 86. What areas are dark? What areas are light? What emotions do these areas suggest?

✏ Which art category best describes **Siegfried and the Rhine Maidens**?
IMITATIONALISM   EMOTIONALISM   FORMALISM

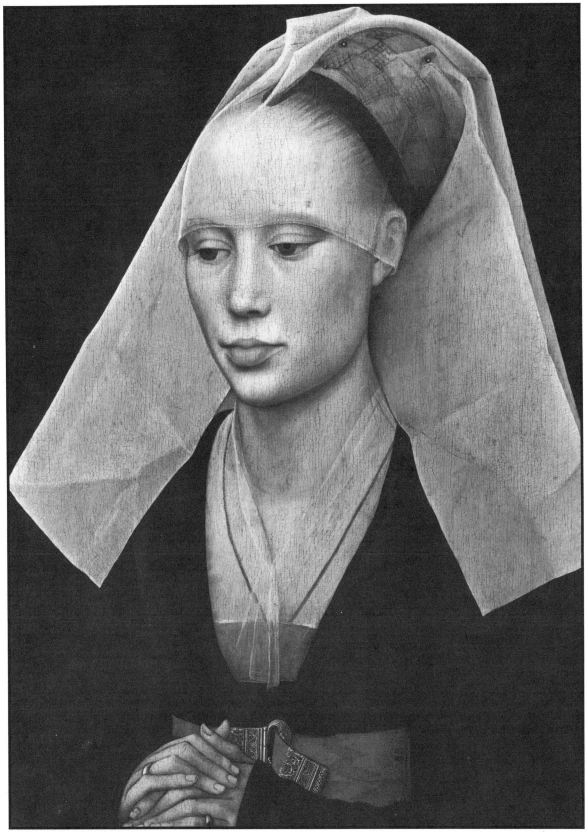

Portrait of a Lady, c. 1460
Rogier van der Weyden

National Gallery of Art
Washington, D.C.

Siegfried and the Rhine Maidens, 1888-91
Albert Pinkham Ryder

National Gallery of Art
Washington, D.C.

In Step 2 of Critiquing Art we have analyzed the ways art elements are arranged in a work of art. We have examined repetition, variation, proximity, focal point, balance, space, and dark and light and how these principles help to form a unified system or design. We are almost ready to discuss the meaning of a work of art.

Look at **Woman Holding a Balance** by Jan Vermeer on p. 88. Pointing out each of the design principles in the painting, discuss how they have been arranged to make a whole.

✏ Which art category best describes **Woman Holding a Balance**?
IMITATIONALISM   EMOTIONALISM   FORMALISM

REVIEW

Use the words in the box below to answer the following questions.

1. A _____ is a scheme of things forming one complete whole.

2. A system consists of a number of _____ that create a whole or _____.

3. The way the elements are put together in a work of art is called the _____,

   or _____.

4. The art elements are _____, _____, _____, and

   _____.

5. The parts of a system are _____. If one part changes, the _____

   changes.

6. The design principle that creates visual rhythm is called _____.

7. The design principle that keeps a design from being boring or monotonous is called

   _____.

8. The _____ is the first thing that attracts your eye in a work of art.

9. The illusion of distance on a flat surface is called _____.

WORD BOX				
system	parts	line	shape	composition
variation	texture	space	whole	interrelated
repetition	unity	design	color	focal point

For answers, see key on p. 112.

Woman Holding a Balance, c. 1664
Jan Vermeer

National Gallery of Art
Washington, D.C.

CRITIQUING ART
Step 3: Interpreting the Meaning

In Step 3 of critiquing a work of art, you will try to discover the theme, or underlying meaning, of the work. To do this you will look at what you have discovered about the art elements and the design and make a guess about the artwork's meaning.

> *The theme and the subject matter of a work of art are not necessarily the same thing. The **theme** is the underlying meaning, or motif, of the work. The **subject matter** includes all the objects you see in the work.*

For example, the subject of **Knight, Death and the Devil** by Albrecht Dürer on p. 29 and **St. George and the Dragon** by Rogier van der Weyden on p. 82 is a knight. But the theme of each painting is very different!

The theme of
Knight, Death and the Devil is
_____ a fun adventure
_____ courage facing death
_____ an interesting design

The theme of
St. George and the Dragon is
_____ the beauty of nature
_____ gallantry and bravery in fighting evil
_____ ways to marry the princess

Understanding a work of art is a little like solving a mystery. To interpret the meaning of a work of art, you examine the clues you have gathered in Steps 1 and 2. Then, make a guess about the meaning.

Look at the drawings below. Using the clues that are provided, make a guess about the meaning of each work.

 In Steps 1 and 2, the artwork at left was described as having sharp, angular lines repeated on a jagged shape in an asymmetrical design. Now, using these clues, decide which is the most likely theme of the artwork:

_____ a happy, pleasant day
_____ a painful, unhappy experience

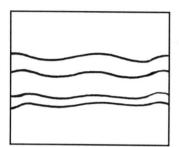 In Steps 1 and 2, the artwork at left was described as having soft, pastel colors floating in lazy, horizontal lines. Now, using these clues, decide which is the most likely theme of the artwork:

_____ a miserable, sad event
_____ a quiet, peaceful time

 In Steps 1 and 2, the artwork at left was described as a person with ornate clothing done in a realistic style in a strongly symmetrical design. Now, using these clues, decide which is the most likely theme of the artwork:

_____ a stately, important person
_____ the plight of the poor

 In Steps 1 and 2, the artwork at left was described as a figure drawn with rough, squiggly lines with superimposed lighter lines. Now, using these clues, decide which is the most likely theme of the artwork:

_____ a serene, calm person
_____ a frightened, haunted person

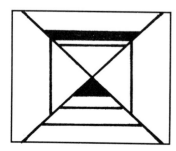 In Steps 1 and 2, the artwork at left was described as a design of blocks of light and dark colors. Now, using these clues, decide which is the most likely theme of the artwork:

_____ mathematical simplicity
_____ the beauty of nature

We will now examine some works of art in detail. You will need 4 separate copies of the three-page Smart Art Worksheet beginning on p. 107. Work through the questions that follow. Remember, we are gathering clues to help us guess what the meaning of each work is.

Grieving by Leonard Baskin on p. 20.

1. First, on the worksheet, classify this work of art according to its primary purpose.
2. Now, under Step 1 on the worksheet, describe as many art elements as you see in the reproduction.
3. Then, under Step 2 on the worksheet, analyze the artwork's design.
4. Finally we are ready for Step 3. Before proceeding with the worksheet, answer the following questions as a way to begin thinking about the meaning of *Grieving:*

   What kind of feeling do the lines give you?
   Why do you think the artist made the figure take up all the space in the work?
   Why does the artist show the figure covering his eyes?
   There is dark around the outside of the figure and light at the top. What might this symbolize?
   Why do the long lines lead toward a focal point at the face?
   The artist chose not to use color. What might this mean?

5. Now, answer the questions under Step 3 on the worksheet, including what you now think the meaning of *Grieving* is.

The Equatorial Jungle by Henri Rousseau on p. 62.

1. First, on the worksheet, classify this work of art according to its primary purpose.
2. Now, under Step 1 on the worksheet, describe as many art elements as you see in the reproduction.
3. Then, under Step 2 on the worksheet, analyze the artwork's design.

4. Finally we are ready for Step 3. Before proceeding with the worksheet, answer the following questions as a way to begin thinking about the meaning of *The Equatorial Jungle*:

What feeling do the light and dark areas of the painting create?
What feeling do the creatures give you?
The painting seems to
_____ have a sense of stillness
_____ have a sense of movement
_____ suggest something is about to happen
_____ suggest things will stay the same
_____ have a dreamlike quality
_____ have a sense of mystery

5. Now, answer the questions under Step 3 on the worksheet, including what you now think the meaning of *The Equatorial Jungle* is.

The Boating Party by Mary Cassatt on p. 42.

1. First, on the worksheet, classify this work of art according to its primary purpose.
2. Now, under Step 1 on the worksheet, describe as many art elements as you see in the reproduction.
3. Then, under Step 2 on the worksheet, analyze the artwork's design.
4. Finally we are ready for Step 3. Before proceeding with the worksheet, answer the following questions as a way to begin thinking about the meaning of ***The Boating Party***:

What are the important shapes in the painting? What feelings to they convey?
The woman seems to be the focal point of the painting. What do you think this means? Is it important that she is holding the child?
The painting seems peaceful. What visual elements create this feeling?
The outline of the boat and the people are very precise. What feeling do these sharp outlines create?

5. Now, answer the questions under Step 3 on the worksheet, including what you now think the meaning of ***The Boating Party*** is.

Still Life: Apples on Pink Tablecloth by Henri Matisse on p. 94.

1. First, on the worksheet, classify this work of art according to its primary purpose.
2. Now, under Step 1 on the worksheet, describe as many art elements as you see in the reproduction.
3. Then, under Step 2 on the worksheet, analyze the artwork's design.
4. Finally we are ready for Step 3. Before proceeding with the worksheet, answer the following questions as a way to begin thinking about the meaning of **Still Life: Apples on Pink Tablecloth:**

   What are the important shapes, lines, and textures in the painting? Do they convey feelings?
   Analyze the design of the painting considering repetition, proximity, balance, and dark and light.
   Is the painting violent or calm? What visual elements create this feeling?
   What is the subject matter of this artwork?

5. Now, answer the questions under Step 3 on the worksheet, including what you now think the meaning of **Still Life: Apples on Pink Tablecloth** is.

National Gallery of Art
Washington, D.C.

CRITIQUING ART
Step 4: Judging the Work

In **SMART ART**, you have learned one method of art criticism. Other methods exist. An important part of this method, however, is that it teaches you to defer judgment. Before judging a work of art, you must do a lot of looking, thinking, and feeling!

Based on all you have learned in Steps 1, 2, and 3, you will now decide whether a work of art is a good example of its kind and, good example or not, you will decide whether you like it.

Name 3 examples in this book of each of the three art categories.	Rank by number the works in each category by how well they achieve their purpose.	Rank by number the works in each category by how much you like them.	Explain why you like your first choices.
IMITATIONALISM			
_____	_____	_____	
_____	_____	_____	
_____	_____	_____	
EMOTIONALISM			
_____	_____	_____	
_____	_____	_____	
_____	_____	_____	
FORMALISM			
_____	_____	_____	
_____	_____	_____	
_____	_____	_____	

Which work of art is your overall favorite? _____
Why?

In Step 3, you discovered the meaning of 4 works of art. It is now time to judge them.

1. Decide which category best describes each work cited below. Choose from imitationalism, emotionalism, or formalism. Any additional thoughts concerning the meaning will also be helpful.

2. Rate each artwork on how well it succeeds. Use the following key for your ratings:

> Outstanding ☆☆☆☆☆
> Very Good ☆☆☆☆
> Good ☆☆☆
> Fair ☆☆
> Poor ☆

The Equatorial Jungle, Henri Rousseau
Art Category _____
Theme_____
My rating in category:

My personal rating:

My thoughts about this artwork:

The Boating Party, Mary Cassatt
Art Category _____
Theme_____
My rating in category:

My personal rating:

My thoughts about this artwork:

Grieving, Leonard Baskin
Art Category _____
Theme_____
My rating in category:

My personal rating:

My thoughts about this artwork:

Still Life: Apples on Pink Tablecloth,
Henri Matisse
Art Category _____
Theme_____
My rating in category:

My personal rating:

My thoughts about this artwork:

YOU BE THE JUDGE

You have learned to defer judgment and to use appropriate criteria to examine works of art. Now it is time to give awards to the deserving. Select your favorites for the awards below. (You can use reproductions from this book or elsewhere.)

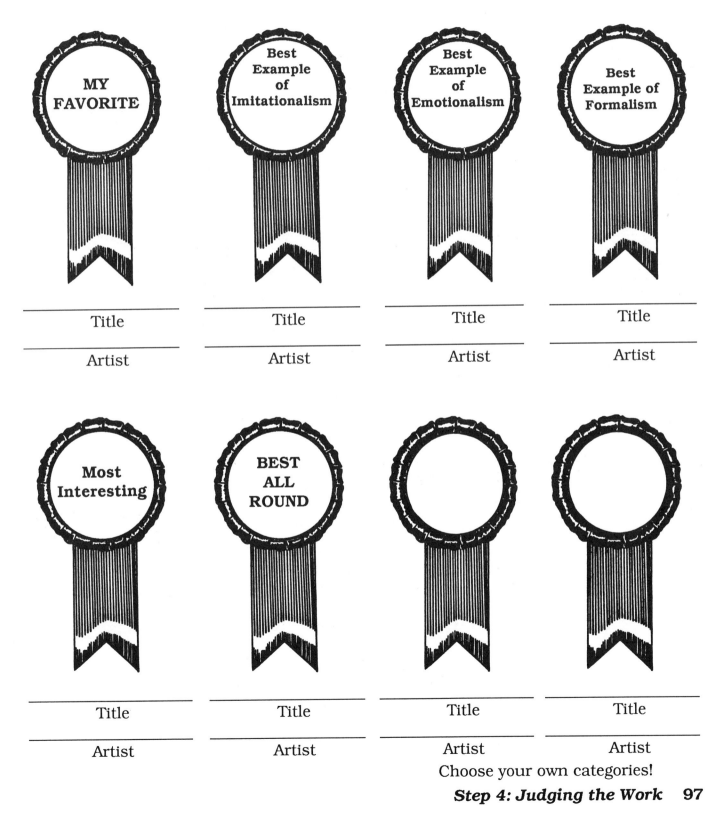

MY FAVORITE	Best Example of Imitationalism	Best Example of Emotionalism	Best Example of Formalism
Title	Title	Title	Title
Artist	Artist	Artist	Artist

Most Interesting	BEST ALL ROUND		
Title	Title	Title	Title
Artist	Artist	Artist	Artist

Choose your own categories!

Name an artist whose work shows:

INTENSITY OF COLOR

1._____

REPETITION OF LINES

2._____

DEEP SPACE

3._____

MOVEMENT

4._____

Art

FANTASY

6._____

SERENITY

5._____

STRONG FOCAL POINT

7._____

DIAGONAL EMPHASIS

8._____

Treasure Hunt

EXCITEMENT

9._____

IMITATIONALISM

10._____

EMOTIONALISM

11._____

FORMALISM

12._____

Which is your favorite?

_____

Why?_____

_____

_____

MORE ACTIVITIES IN ART CRITICISM

This section contains reproductions of three works of art along with the name of each artist, the date of composition, information on the subject of the work and the materials used, and several questions designed to make you think about each work.

The exercises will give you additional experience in classifying and critiquing art, and you will become familiar with three famous works of art! The works included are:

David and Bathsheba, Pablo Picasso

Dark and Red Carp, Shoson Ohara

A Commentary on a Living Standard, Michitada Kono

David and Bathsheba, 1947
Pablo Picasso

University of Oregon Museum of Art
Eugene, Oregon

David and Bathsheba, 1947, Pablo Picasso
Lithograph

David and Bathsheba is a story from the Old Testament of the Bible. David, the king, is falling in love with Bathsheba, who is married to one of David's generals. From his tower where he is playing the harp, King David can see Bathsheba bathing. A lithograph is a picture made from a flat, specially prepared stone or plate. More than one copy of the same image can be made using this process.

Use another sheet if necessary to answer the following questions:

1. Which art classification best describes this lithograph?

2. Why do you think some of the figures are barely sketched in and others have more detail? What does it mean that King David has facial features and darkened hair and robe? How does the bottom half of the lithograph contrast with the top half?

3. What shapes are used to draw Bathsheba? How is she different from the woman washing her feet?

4. Why is King David's tower so angular and crooked? What does this mean to you?

5. What are the focal points in the lithograph?

6. Does King David look interested in playing his harp? Where are his eyes looking? What might be on his mind?

7. What might the dark shadows mean?

8. What do the expressions on the women's faces tell you?

9. What is your first impression of the lithograph? Does it change as you look at it more carefully?

10.What do you think Picasso was trying to do in this lithograph?

Dark and Red Carp, n.d.
Shoson Ohara

University of Orgeon Museum of Art
Eugene, Oregon

Dark and Red Carp, n.d., Shoson Ohara
Woodblock print

The bright flat colors and simple design of Japanese art has influenced many artists, particularly the Impressionists in Europe at the turn of the century. A woodblock print is a picture made from a block of wood that has been carved into by the artist. The raised portion of the wood is covered with ink and the paper is pressed over it, transferring the image from the woodblock to the paper. More than one copy of the same image can be made using this process.

Use another sheet if necessary to answer the following questions:

1. Which art classification best describes this print?

2. What lines and shapes do you see repeated?

3. What visual textures are created?

4. How does the artist make the large fish the focal point of this print?

5. How is proximity and overlapping used in this print?

6. How does the artist create a feeling of space? How does the artist show us that objects are under water?

7. How many shades of gray do you see?

8. Think of five single words to describe this print.

9. What do you think Ohara was trying to do in this print?

A Commentary on a Living Standard, 1953
Michitada Kono

University of Oregon Museum of Art
Eugene, Oregon

A Commentary on a Living Standard, 1953, Michitada Kono
Oil on canvas

This is a painting of tofu-making. Tofu is a soft, bland, cheeselike food made from curdled soybean milk. In Japan, tofu is as important as bread is to us, so the artist has created an important but common scene. An oil painting is made by covering a canvas surface with layers of oil paints. The paints are made by mixing ground pigments with just enough oil to make them sticky.

Use another sheet if necessary to answer the following questions:

1. Which art classification best describes this painting?

2. What is the focal point of this painting? What kind of balance is used?

3. What shapes do you see?

4. Where are the light and dark areas? Where does it look like light is coming from in this painting? What kind of light do you think it is?

5. Why do you think the artist painted such an ordinary scene? What does the title mean to you?

6. What could you draw that would show our standard of living?

7. What do you think Kono was trying to do in this painting?

THE NEXT STEP . . . ○ ○ ○

Now that you have completed the activities in **SMART ART**, you are ready to take the next step! Using all that you have learned about classifying and critiquing art, you can now look at works of art anywhere and talk about them knowledgeably.

To help you apply all that you have learned, a Smart Art Worksheet is included on the following three pages. It provides a checklist to help you through the various steps outlined in **SMART ART**. It may be photocopied and used whenever you wish to examine a work of art.

Here are a few suggestions to help you begin the next step:

- Make a copy of the Smart Art Worksheet and use it to examine a reproduction from the front or back cover of this book. If you cannot make a new copy of the worksheet, use a separate sheet of paper for your answers.

- Share **SMART ART** with a brother, a sister, or a friend. They will be very impressed with how much you know about art!

- Ask a teacher, a parent, or your librarian to help you find other works of art to examine. You may have several art books at home or you may find one in your local library. Using the Smart Art Worksheet, examine any reproduction in the book you find interesting.

- Ask a teacher or a parent to help you visit a local museum. Original works of art are much more interesting to examine in person. Remember to take along a copy of the Smart Art Worksheet!

- Examine a work of art with your family, your friends, or another group of people. You may have to lead the discussion!

- Take your family or friends to a museum and examine the original works of art. You may need the worksheet to start the process.

Congratulations! You have learned a lot about classifying and critiquing art. Hope you enjoy examining the many works of art all around us. Have fun!

Smart Art Worksheet

Title of the artwork:_____

Name of the artist:_____

Date:_____

The primary purpose of this work of art is
  to imitate nature (imitationalism) ___
  to show a feeling or emotion (emotionalism) ___
  to make the viewer aware of lines, shapes, colors, or design (formalism) ___

STEP 1: The art elements—Describe what you see in the painting.

LINES—What kinds of lines do you see?

sharp ___	fuzzy ___
thick ___	thin ___
jagged ___	curved ___
heavy ___	graceful ___
choppy___	smooth ___
vertical ___	horizontal ___
diagonal ___	straight ___
other	other

_____ _____

TEXTURES—What kinds of textures do you see?

rough ___	soft ___
smooth ___	hard ___
shiny ___	dull ___
other	other

_____ _____

SHAPES—What kinds of shapes do you see?

circles ___	squares ___
rectangles ___	triangles ___
curved ___	angular ___
soft-edged ___	hard-edged ___
other _____	other _____

COLORS—What kinds of colors do you see?

bright ___	warm colors	complementary colors
soft ___	reds ___	blues and oranges ___
dark ___	oranges ___	reds and greens ___
strong ___	yellows ___	yellows and purples___
	cool colors	neutral colors
	blues ___	browns ___ grays ___
	greens ___	whites ___
	purples ___	

OBJECTS—What kinds of objects do you see?

young people ___	boats ___	sky ___
old people ___	animals ___	rocks ___
buildings ___	trees ___	water ___
food ___	musical instruments ___	

there are no objects ___

other _____

other _____

STEP 2:
The design—Look at the way the art elements are put together.

REPETITION—What do you see repeated in the painting?

lines ___ Draw the kind you see repeated most.

shapes ___ Draw the kind you see repeated most.

colors ___ Name the colors you see most.

PROXIMITY—How close together are the objects or elements you see?

Do some objects or elements overlap others?

SPACE—What kind of space is used?

deep space ___
(looks like you can see for miles)

shallow space ___
(you cannot see very far)

BALANCE--What kind of balance is used?
symmetrical ____
(each side of the painting is similar)

asymmetrical ____
(each side of the painting is different)

radial ____
(elements branch out from a common point)

VARIATION—What variation do you see in the painting?

lines ___ Draw the various lines you see.

shapes ___ Draw the various shapes you see.

colors ___ Name the various colors you see.

FOCAL POINT— What is the first thing you see when you look at the painting?

LIGHT—Squint and look at the painting. Where do you see the most light areas?

right side ___   center ___
left side ___   top ___
bottom ___

DARK—Squint and look at the painting. Where do you see the most dark areas?

right side _____   center _____
left side _____   top _____
bottom _____

STEP 3:
Meaning—What is the meaning of the work of art?

Now, go back and reread how you described the art elements in Step 1. What effect do they create? Reread how you described the design in Step 2. What effect does it create? These are clues to the meaning of the painting and will help you answer the following questions:

I originally classified this work of art as an example of
imitationalism ___ emotionalism ___ formalism ___ .

I have ___/have not ___ changed my opinion.

I think the primary purpose of this work is to
imitate nature ___ express emotion ___ show creative design ___.

Does the title of the work of art tell you about the meaning? Yes ___ No ___

Which of the following words would help you describe this work of art?

strength ___	hate ___	enjoyment of work ___
beauty ___	anger ___	death ___
love ___	adventure ___	interest in shapes ___
madness ___	interest in lines ___	mystery ___
excitement ___	simplicity of design ___	war ___
courage ___	complexity of design ___	happiness ___
horror ___	loneliness ___	old age ___
fear ___	peace ___	fun ___
hope ___	sadness ___	interest in color ___
other _____	other _____	other _____

Now that I have examined the art elements, analyzed the design, and considered the purpose of the work, I am ready to make a knowledgeable guess about the meaning of the work of art. I think in this painting the artist was trying to:

_____

STEP 4: Judgment—Judge the painting.

This painting is an excellent ___ good ___ bad ___ example of
imitationalism ___ emotionalism ___ formalism ___ .

I like ___ don't like ___ this artwork.

GLOSSARY

Analogous colors: colors next to each other on the color wheel.

Asymmetrical balance: when opposite sides of a work of art are balanced not by matching elements but by elements that attract the eye equally.

Background: the part of a work of art that looks farthest away from the viewer.

Balance: achieved in a work of art when opposite sides contain elements of equal weight. There are three types of balance: symmetrical, asymmetrical, and radial.

Collage: a work created by pasting together paper, cloth, or other materials on a surface.

Color: the way we see light reflected from a surface or refracted through a prism.

Color wheel: a tool artists use to arrange colors in a circle to show how each color is related to the others.

Complementary colors: opposite colors on the color wheel.

Composition: the way art elements are put together in a work of art. Also called design.

Cool colors: usually considered to be green, blue, and purple.

Dark and light: The use of shadow and light to create visual interest in a work of art. Sometimes dark areas are used to contrast sharply with light areas.

Deep space: the illusion of great distance on a flat surface.

Design: the way art elements are put together in a work of art. Also called composition.

Elements: the lines, shapes, colors, and textures that an artist uses to create a work of art.

Emotionalism: a category used to classify art when the primary purpose of the work is to express strong feelings, moods, or ideas.

Focal point: the first thing that attracts the eye to a work of art. The focal point is often what the artist wants to emphasize most.

Foreground: the part of a work of art that appears closest to the viewer. This is often the most important part of the work.

Formalism: a category used to classify art when the primary purpose of the work is to create a visually interesting experience.

Hue: another name for color. For example, red, red-orange, orange, orange-yellow, and yellow are all hues.

Illusion: something that appears different from what it actually is.

Imitationalism: a category used to classify art when the primary purpose of a work is to imitate the physical world around us.

Impasto: created when paint is applied so heavily that it stands up in lumps.

Intensity: the brightness of a color.

Line: the path created by a moving dot.

Lithograph: an image produced in multiples from a flat, specially prepared stone or metal plate.

Mosaic: a work of art made of many pieces of colored tiles or stones arranged in a pattern or picture.

Motif: the underlying meaning or theme of a work of art.

Objects: the identifiable things you see in a picture that help you know both the subject matter and theme.

Oil on canvas: a work of art made by covering a canvas surface with layers of oil paints. The paints are made by mixing ground pigments with oil to make them sticky and spreadable.

Overlapping: placing one object or shape over another so that only a portion of the one behind is showing.

Pattern: the effect created by repeating similar objects and elements over and over.

Pigment: substances used to give color. Originally, pigments included natural materials like walnut shells, carrots, and berries. Today, most pigments are manufactured.

Primary colors: red, yellow, blue. They are called primary colors because all other colors are made from them.

Proximity: how close together objects or elements are.

Radial balance: when all the elements of a work of art branch out in all directions from a common point.

Repetition: the use of an object or element over and over again. In a work of art, repetition creates visual rhythm.

Reproduction: in art, a photograph or other copy made from an original work of art. The originals of most of the reproductions in this book are in color.

Secondary colors: purple, green, and orange. They are called secondary colors because they are made from mixing two of the primary colors.

Shade: the darkness of a color achieved by adding black.

Shallow space: the illusion of little or no space on a flat surface.

Shape: created when a line encloses a space or when a line separates one area from another.

Space: in a work of art, illusion of distance on a flat surface.

Subject matter: all the objects seen in a work of art.

Symbol: something used to represent something else. A dove, for example, is often used to represent peace.

Symmetrical balance: when opposite sides of a work of art are balanced by matching elements.

System: a set of parts that creates a whole.

Tactile texture: the way a surface feels.

Theme: the underlying meaning or motif of a work of art.

Tint: the lightness of a color achieved by adding white.

Unity: a whole created by grouping a number of parts.

Value: the lightness or darkness of a color.

Variation: a partial change in the way an object or element is repeated. In a work of art, variation creates visual interest.

Visual texture: the way a surface looks like it would feel, although the surface is actually smooth. Artists create the illusion of visual texture on a flat surface.

Warm colors: usually considered to be red, orange, and yellow.

Woodblock print: created by carving into a block of wood, inking the raised portion, and pressing paper onto the wood, permitting multiple images to be made.

ANSWER KEY

pp. 31-33	1. imitationalism 2. emotionalism 3. imitationalism 4. formalism 5. emotionalism 6. formalism
p. 54	1. line, color, shape, texture 2. dot 3. area 4. shape 5. distance, balance, wholeness 6. light 7. red, yellow, blue 8. secondary, primary 9. complementary, red/green, purple/yellow 10. red, orange, yellow 11. green, blue, purple 12. any three colors 13. berries 14. tactile 15. mosaic 16. visual
p. 55	1. shape 2. color 3. line 4. texture
p. 87	1. system 2. parts, unity 3. design, composition 4. line, shape, color, texture 5. interrelated, whole 6. repetition 7. variation 8. focal point 9. space

---

For a complete line of learning materials that foster whole-brain learning, creative and critical thinking, and self-awareness, send for a free catalog:

Zephyr Press
P.O. Box 66006
Tucson, AZ 85728-6006